Islam
Riadh El Droubie

Ward Lock Educational

ISBN 0 7062 3595 9
First published 1970
Reprinted 1971
Reprinted January 1973
Reprinted November 1973

© Ward Lock Educational 1970. All rights reserved. No part of this publication may be reproduced, stored in a retrieval system, or transmitted, in any form or by any means, electronic, mechanical, photo-copying, recording or otherwise, without the prior permission of the Copyright owner.

Set in 11 on 12 point Press Roman on an IBM 72 Composer
for Ward Lock Educational Company Limited
116 Baker Street, London W1M 2BB

Printed in Spain by Editorial fher s.a.

Contents

Acknowledgments 4

1 **How Islam began**
   Arabia before Islam 5
   Muhammad the prophet 6

2 **What Muslims believe**
   Belief 9
   Action 11
   Prayer 12
   The daily prayers 13
   The mosque 17
   The Holy Qur'an 19
   The story of creation 21
   Sin 21
   Different schools of thought within Islam 21

3 **How Muslims live**
   Zakat 22
   The pilgrimage to Mecca 23
   Fasting 23
   The Islamic calendar 23
   Feasts and holidays 24
   Marriage and divorce 26
   Polygamy 26
   Prohibitions 27
   Muslims and people of other religions 27

   Suggestions for further reading 29
   Index 30

Acknowledgments

The author and publishers wish to thank the following for their help in providing the photographs and drawings which illustrate this book:
The British Museum p 10; Elizabeth Clarke pp 6, 24, 27; Robin Kempster who took the photographs on pp 15, 16; Keystone Press Agency p 25 top; Paul Popper pp 13, 17, 18, 19, 20, 22, 23, 25 bottom.

1 How Islam began

Islam is the religion which was revealed to the prophet Muhammad in Arabia in the year 610 AD when he was forty years of age.

The word *Islam* is the Arabic name for the religion of the prophet Ibrahim meaning in this case submission to the Will of God and the observance of His Command. It also means peace – peace with God and with one's fellowman. Peace with God implies complete submission to His Will, for He is the source of all purity and goodness. Peace with other people means not just refraining from evil or injury to others but positively doing good.

Muslims dislike the name Mohammadan given to them by non Muslims because they believe that Muhammad was a prophet and a man. He was not the founder of the religion of Islam, but a messenger of God who carried out his duties as he was commanded; he was neither God, nor a son of God.

Arabia before Islam

Arabia was separated from the neighbouring countries by an ocean of sand. So it had received nothing from the civilizations around it, but stood isolated. There were a few literate men, but they were not sufficiently interested or educated to be able to develop their society. The only law which existed was tribal law which depended entirely upon the decisions of the tribe leader. The whole land was in a state of chaos and a quarrel between two individuals was enough to cause a war all over Arabia.

So we can see that in pre-Islamic times, the social and political life of Arabia was at a very low level. Superstition and idolatry existed everywhere. The people worshipped idols made of stone and wood, and some worshipped the stars and believed in the spirits. Life was barbaric; the Arabs used to go naked when they performed their ceremonies around the sacred Ka'ba which contained their idols and their only skills were riding horses, fighting, using the Arabic language and above all their famous hospitality.

All the wealth of Mecca the central city of Arabia, came from the pilgrims who arrived every year. Since Mecca was surrounded by mountains and desert nothing grew there so all the necessities of life were brought by camel caravans from the north, particularly from Syria, Jordan and Egypt. In this way Mecca became not only the centre of religious activities in pre-Islamic Arabia, but of commerce for the whole of western Asia.

There were a few other religions in Arabia, but they were only a small minority. Fire worship came from Persia, Judaism came with those who fled from the Romans and Christianity came from the Eastern Church. In spite of these religions the majority of people in Arabia practised idolatry, believing that their idols could bring them near to the creator and could also perform miracles. However, they also accepted the Jewish and Christian belief in the new prophet who would come to their land and worship the same God of Abraham who built the sacred Ka'ba at Mecca.

The sacred Ka'ba is a rectangular stone building 8 metres high which is covered with black brocade

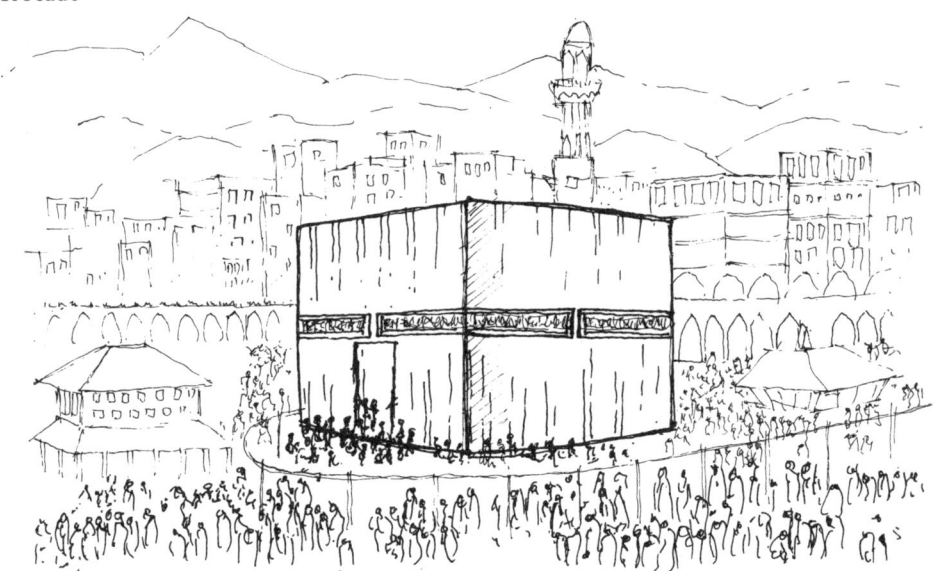

Muhammad the Prophet

The Arabs are the descendants of the prophet Ishmael, son of the prophet Abraham. Later they split into many tribes and became idolaters. The Quraish were the strongest among the tribes and occupied a position of honour as custodians of the Ka'ba.

In the year 570 AD on the 12th of the month *Rabi-ul-Awwal* of the Arabian calendar, a child was born to Abdullah, son of Abdul Muttalib of the Quraish tribe in Mecca. But Abdullah was not fortunate enough to see his newborn son as he died before his birth.

The Holy Qur'an describes how at that time the Abyssinian king had sent his army with elephants in an attempt to destroy the Ka'ba. The Arabs were not familiar with elephant warfare and so were unable to resist the invaders, but the invading army was miraculously destroyed by birds sent by God and the Ka'ba was saved.

According to the custom of wealthy Arabian people at that time, Muhammad was brought up in the desert away from towns. His mother died when he was six and his grandfather then took care of him. His grandfather loved him dearly and always kept him at his side but he died two years later when Muhammad was eight and his uncle Abu Talib then looked after him.

Abu Talib was a trader who frequently travelled to Syria. When Muhammad was twelve years old his uncle started on a journey to Syria and Muhammad accompanied him. When they reached half way, Abu Talib lodged with a Christian monk named Bahira who when he saw Muhammad exclaimed, 'This is the greatest prophet!' Abu Talib asked him how he knew this and the monk replied, 'I saw a cloud coming with you and it stopped on your caravan.' Then he examined the child's body and discovered the seal of prophethood between his shoulder blades. Because of this the monk feared that some harm might come to the child and asked his uncle to turn back towards Mecca. Abu Talib accepted his advice, abandoned the journey to Syria and returned to Mecca.

Muhammad was called *Al-Amin*, which means trustworthy. He was famous for his honesty and his opinion was highly respected and accepted by the people. It was decided that the Ka'ba should be repaired and when the work was completed, a quarrel broke out among the different tribes about who should lift the black stone and set it in its place. The quarrel had lasted a few days when one member proposed that the dispute be decided by the first man who came to the Ka'ba the following morning. This proposal was accepted by all. Muhammad was the first man to arrive that morning and the people were all glad to see him. He spread out a robe and placed the black stone upon it and then asked the heads of the various tribes to each hold a corner and lift up the stone together. In this way the stone was carried to its proper place and much bloodshed was avoided.

A wealthy merchant's widow called Khadija heard of Muhammad's honesty. She sent him an offer — if he would manage her trading caravan, she would pay him more than she had paid others. He accepted and went to Syria with her merchandise, where he was very successful in making a good profit. Khadija was delighted with his success and honesty and when he returned she sent him a marriage proposal. They were married when he was twenty-five and she was forty.

Muhammad often needed to get away from people and he used to go off into the desert where he liked to think and meditate about the Creator and life. The Cave of Hira'a on Mount Light (Jabal-al-Noor) was his favourite retreat.

One day while he was in the cave meditating an angel came to him and said 'Read!' 'I cannot read', replied Muhammad. The angel took him firmly in his arms and repeated three times, 'Read!' Then the angel started reading and Muhammad read after him. The angel then disappeared. That was the first of the revealed Qur'an and it goes as follows:

In the name of Allah, the Beneficent, the Merciful
Read in the name of thy Lord who created
Man from a clot of Blood
Read! Thy Lord is most Generous,
Who taught by the pen,
Taught man what he knew not.
Nay, man is surely inordinate,
Because he looks upon himself as independent.
Surely to thy Lord all things return.
Hast thou seen him who rebukes
A servant when he prays?
Seest thou if he is on (the road of) guidance
Or enjoins righteousness?
Seest thou if he denies and turns away?
Knows he not that Allah sees?
Nay, if he desist not, We will seize him by the forelock,
A lying, sinful forelock!
Then let him summon his helpmates.
We will call the guards of hell.
Nay! Obey not thou him. But prostrate thyself,
And draw near unto Allah. (Surah 96)

Muhammad was frightened and went home trembling. He told his wife Khadija of what had happened in the cave, and she told him she was sure it was the archangel Gabriel and urged him to go with her to visit her uncle Waraka, a learned man who had accepted Christianity and who might be able to tell them the meaning of it. After Waraka learned what happened, he told them that Muhammad was the prophet about whom they had been told in the ancient books.

For three years Muhammad kept his religion a secret which he shared with only a few friends. Then God sent him the message to preach so that mankind would give up its evil ways and follow in the straight path of Allah. Muhammad stood on the hill of Safa in the centre of Mecca and proclaimed the message of God, inviting the people to join him.

He was forty when he became a prophet, and after twenty-three years of prophetic life he died in 632 AD in Medina, the second sacred city of Islam. The news of his death was announced by his caliph Abu Bakr in these words: 'Let him know, whosoever worshipped Muhammad, that Muhammad is dead; but whosoever worshipped God, let him know that God lives and never dies.'

2 What Muslims believe

Islam is built upon two important foundations — belief and action. Neither belief nor action by themselves are enough. The prophet Muhammad said: *Islam is built on many pillars; the best of them is bearing witness that there is no God but one God and Muhammad is His Messenger, and the lowest of them is the removal from the path of that which is harmful.*

Belief

A Muslim must believe in one God, His Angels, His Books, His Prophets, the Day of Judgment, the good and evil of fate and life after death.

A Muslim believes in one God who is the only one worthy of worship, the Almighty, the All Knowing, the All Just, the Loving, the Merciful. He begets neither son nor daughter and is not begotten. He is the Light of Heaven and Earth, and He is the First, the Last and the Eternal.

The angels are created of light and given life. They are free of desire, never disobey and do all that they are commanded. There are four archangels: Gabriel who brings the revelations of God to the prophets, Michael who brings the rain, Israfil who calls for the Day of Judgment and Azrail the angel of death.

It is understood by Muslims that God has revealed many messages and commandments to various prophets at different times in different places. The last four holy books which were revealed are: the *Taurant* (Old Testament) to Moses; the *Zaboor* (Psalms) to David; the *Injeel* (New Testament) to Jesus; the *Qur'an* to Muhammad. Muslims believe that the first three books do not exist in their original forms. The present day editions are only interpretations by their followers of later ages.

The Qur'an is the Book of Islam which was revealed to the prophet Muhammad during the last twenty-three years of his life, either as single sentences or paragraphs which were written down at his directions and arranged under his supervision during his lifetime.

In ancient times God sent many messengers and prophets to guide mankind to the right way. Some of them were mentioned in the Qur'an for their importance, and some were not. The Qur'an says:
Say (O Muslims): We believe in Allah and that which is revealed unto us and that which was revealed unto

Abraham, and Ishmael, and Isaac, and Jacob, and the tribes, and that which Moses and Jesus received, and that which the Prophets received from their Lord. We make no distinction between any of them, and unto Him we have surrendered. (Surah 2 v. 136)

Muhammad is seen as the last but not the only prophet of God. Muslims

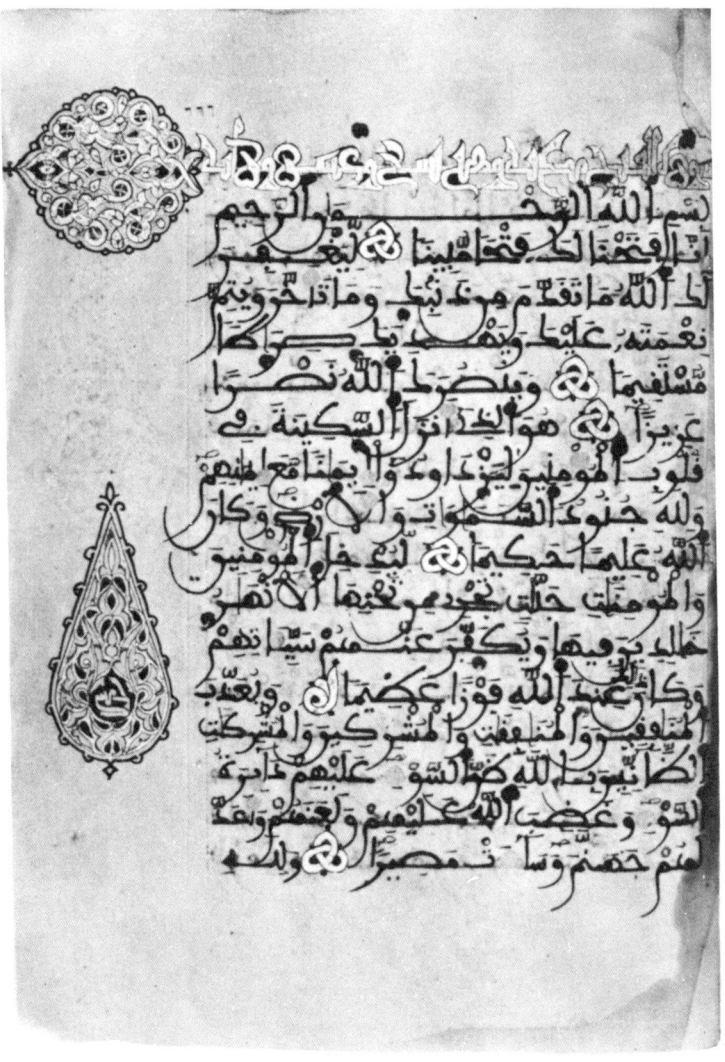

A page from the Qur'an containing the beginning of Surah 48

do not worship any of the prophets, but they do love them and consider them as examples and models for mankind. None of them was divine, but all were servants of God and human.

All the holy books as originally revealed by God have been lost and exist only in altered form, except for the Holy Qur'an, which will be preserved in its original form by God for all time to come. Because of this there is no need for a new message and no need for a new prophet; Muhammad is the final messenger and the Qur'an is the final message of God.

On the Day of Judgment the dead will be resurrected and their deeds will be counted. Muslims believe that actions will be judged according to intentions. God will reward the righteous by peace and happiness in heaven, and those who disobeyed Him will go to hell. Everybody will be rewarded or punished according to what they have done.

God has given man the power of doing good and bad and has sent down messages through the prophets and messengers to show man the right path. As man has the power to choose between good and evil he is responsible for what he says. God will be the only judge when we stand before Him on the Day of Judgment and He alone can forgive. The prophet Muhammad himself will not be able to help even his own daughter on that day. God will grant forgiveness if a man prays to Him without the help of a priest or the prayers of another pious man and promises not to commit the same bad action again.

Action

Action or practice in Islam is as important as belief itself. Muslims believe that each person is responsible for his own deeds and he will answer for them on the Day of Judgment. Most important of all in Islam is the intention, for actions are judged by the intention and not by the result. There are two kinds of action; general practice or duties towards others, and compulsory duties towards God.

Where duties towards others are concerned the Holy Qur'an repeats the call to Muslims to do good: *O you who believe and do good!*, it also says: *Kind speech and forgiveness are better than charity followed by injury.* Truth, justice and good behaviour are all good and accepted as good by the general moral code of humanity. The religion of Islam came to purify the nature of man, so a true Muslim must adapt his life to this moral code and the teachings of Islam. He must not lie and he must help others, even if they are not Muslims. But that is not all; if he sees evil, he must tell others about it and help them to avoid it. If he sees good things, he must tell others about it and encourage them to do good. The most humble of good actions is to remove from the path of other people anything which is harmful, like stones or pieces of glass.

The whole life of a Muslim is dedicated to the worship of God; wordly actions cannot be separated from religious deeds. In every action we must seek the pleasure of God, even in our work at school. If we are sincere and try to do our best God will be pleased with us; but if we are careless and fail to do the best we can God will be displeased with us. Every man, woman and child whether Muslim or not is expected to be truthful, helpful and kind and to do his very best.

Compulsory duties are for Muslims only. The prophet Muhammad said *Islam is built on five pillars: bearing witness that there is no God but (one) God and Muhammad is His Messenger; being steadfast in prayer; paying the zakat; the pilgrimage to Mecca and fasting during the month of Ramadan.*

The formal declaration of faith (*Shahadah*) states the first principle in Islam — that there is no deity but God and Muhammad is the apostle of God; *I bear witness that there is no God but one God and I bear witness that Muhammad is His Messenger.* This means that there is none worthy of worship but God. He has no partner. He gives life and causes death and He begets not, nor is He begotten; and there is none like Him.

A person becomes a Muslim as soon as he makes submission to God. The formal declaration of faith *(Shahadah)* must be said in front of an authority and at least one adult Muslim witness. Before doing so a ritual bath must be taken. From now on the five daily prayers are compulsory.

Prayer

Of the five pillars in Islam, prayer takes second place after the declaration of faith. A Muslim must first believe and then submit himself to God by keeping up his daily prayers. Muslims pray to submit themselves to destiny and to adore the divine greatness of God — also to find moral strength for themselves and society.

Prayers may be divided into two types: *Du'ah* meaning petition or invocation which implies that man in this world is weak and helpless without the mercy and grace of God. These prayers may be performed at any time and anywhere. *Salat* is the name given to the prescribed worship with ritual movements which must be performed five times a day at fixed times. To perform the Salat you must be fully conscious, clear in mind and clean in body and dress. These prayers are compulsory for men and women over the age of ten and may be performed alone or in congregation.

Before prayers a Muslim must clean himself in the prescribed manner known as *Wudhu* (ablution). This consists of repeating *In the name of God the Beneficent, the Merciful* while washing the hands with pure water up to the wrists three times, rinsing the mouth, with a toothbrush if possible, three times, rinsing the nose, face, right arm and left arm to the elbow three times, passing wet hands over the head ears and neck, and finally washing the right and then left foot to the ankle three times.

Having finished his ablutions a Muslim must stand on clean ground at the prescribed times, face in the direction of Mecca and call for prayer saying:

Allahu-Akbar (four times) God is the greatest

Ash-ahdu-an-la-ilaha-illalah (twice) I bear witness that there is no God but Allah

Ash-hado anna mohammadan-rasulullah (twice) I bear witness that Mohammad is the messenger of Allah

Hayye-alas-salah (twice) Come to prayer

Hayye-alal-falah (twice) Come to security

Allahu-Akbar (twice) God is the greatest

La-illah-illalah (once) There is no God but Allah

The daily prayers

Before the beginning of each set of daily prayers in the mosque, the *muezzin* goes up into one of the minarets of the mosque and calls the faithful to prayer crying 'God is the greatest. I bear witness that there is no God but Allah. I bear witness that Muhammad is the messenger of Allah. Come to prayer. Come to security. God is the greatest.'

The muezzin standing in the minaret calls the faithful to prayer in Tunisia

Once inside the mosque the congregation take up their positions facing Mecca. Each person decides for himself the number of rak'as (sets of vital prayer movements) individually performed and then the prescribed prayer begin led by the Imam (prayer leader) as prescribed by the Prophet Muhammad.

The rak'ah is begun by lifting the hands to the ears and saying 'God is the greatest'. The position is then changed by placing the right hand on top of the left and placing both just above the navel. The words recited after this movement are those of the opening chapter of the Qur'an, and any other short *sura* (chapter) or three *ayyats* (verses) from the Qur'an.

The opening chapter of the Qur'an
All praise be to God, Lord of the Worlds
The Beneficent, the Merciful
The Lord of the Day of Judgment
Thee alone we worship and Thee alone we seek help from
Guide us to the straight path
The path of those whom Thou hast favoured
Not the path of those who incur Thine anger
Nor of those who go astray Amen
Al-hamdu lillahi rabbil alamin
Ar-rahmanu ar-raheem
Maliki yaumideen
E-yaka na'a-budu wa e-yaka nasta'een
Ehdinas-siratal-mustaqeem
Siratal-latheen an-amta alayhin
Ghairil-Maghdoobi Alayhim
Wa-la-dal-leen Amen (Sura 1)

The Unity Sura
Say: God is One
The eternal God
He begets not nor is He begotten
And there is none like him
Qul Huwal-lahu Ahed
Al-Lahus-samad
Lam yalid wa lam yolad
Wa lam yakun Lahu Kufuwan Ahad (Sura 112)

With the words *Allahu Akbar* the position changes to a bowing movement, with hands on knees and legs kept straight repeating three times *Subhana Rabiyal-Adeem* — All glory to God the greatest. Then standing upright the following words are spoken: *Sami 'al-'Lahu Limen hamidah Rab-bana*

Lakal-Hamd — God has listened to him who has praised Him our God: Praise be to Thee. The worshipper then prostrates himself, sinking to his knees and placing his hands on the ground and putting his nose and forehead between them on the ground repeating three times *Subhana Rabiyal-a'a-la* — All glory to God the highest. Swinging back onto his heels he says *Allahuma Egh-fir-lee war-hamnie* — O God forgive me and have mercy upon me, and then prostrates himself a second time repeating the words which accompanied the first prostration. This completes the first rak'ah. Once the number of rak'as have been performed the *Tashahud* and *Du'ah* are recited and the ceremony is completed by saying *Assalamu 'alaikum wa rahmatullah* — Peace be upon you and the mercy of God. During the speaking of these words the head is turned to look once over the right and once over the left shoulder.

The rak'ah begins by lifting the hands to the ears. The second movement is to place the right hand on the left and place both just above the navel. The third position, a bowing movement with hands placed on the knees, can be seen on page 23. The worshipper then stands upright as shown below

The worshipper then prostrates himself twice to complete the first rak'ah

When all the rak'as have been performed the ceremony is completed by turning the head to look once over the right shoulder and then over the left

    A Muslim has to pray two rak'as at dawn, four at midday, four in the afternoon, three just after sunset and four ninety minutes after sunset.

    Friday is a public holiday in Muslim countries. Muslims do believe that God created heaven and earth in six days but believe that God did not need any rest on the seventh day. Friday prayers are held in the mosque, and the midday prayer is replaced by a congregational service when the Imam delivers a sermon followed by two rak'as.

The mosque

The mosque (place of prostration) acts as a focal point for Muslims' devotions. It must have some sort of court and fountains to provide pure water for the ablutions which every Muslim has to perform before prayer.

Inside the mosque there is generally an air of great serenity and peace. It has certain important features such as a pulpit, a lectern carrying a copy of the Holy Qur'an and a mihrab which is the equivalent of an altar. The mihrab is a small recess shaped like a semicircle facing in the direction of Mecca. All Muslims face the mihrab during prayers.

Women are not prohibited from attending services in the mosque but are advised not to because of their responsibilities at home. Nowadays women do attend services in most Muslim countries and often special quarters in the mosques are built for them.

The Sultan Hamed mosque in Istanbul

The court and ablution fountain of a mosque in Cairo

The beautifully decorated mihrab in what was once the cathedral of the Holy Wisdom, became a mosque in 1453, and is now a museum

The Holy Qur'an

The Holy Qur'an is the word of God revealed to the last prophet Muhammad through the archangel Gabriel in Arabic. The Qur'an consists of 114 chapters or sura containing over 6,200 verses or ayyats. There is no doubt as to its authenticity and originality. It was revealed in parts, either in small verses or in sections, and the prophet Muhammad appointed special writers to record the revelations under his supervision.

A Muslim sits reading the Qur'an in a mosque in New Delhi

The Arab of the desert has a great gift for memorizing poetry and this has helped Muslims to learn the Qur'an by heart. After the death of the prophet, war broke out and this led to the slaughter of a large number of people who had memorized the Qur'an. To prevent any likelihood of the Qur'an disappearing the first caliph Abu Bakr ordered several experts from among the Muslims to compile a standard copy of the Qur'an which was checked by several different authorities. Fifteen years after the prophet's death the third caliph ordered additional copies to be made and distributed it to other territories under Islamic rule.

The Qur'an plays a very special part in the lives of most Muslims who have to recite a section or verses from it five times a day in their prayers, and try to learn as many verses as possible by heart. It can be a source of great comfort in times of hardship and seems to have an appropriate verse for every occasion. No pious Muslim would ever smoke, drink or make a noise while it was being read aloud. Most important of all the Qur'an is the foundation of all Islamic legislation and is used as the basis for the Islamic way of life.

The story of creation
The Qur'an says: *God it was who created the heavens and the earth and that which is between them in six days.* (Sura 32) This is understood by Muslims to mean that God's work did not end with creating heaven and earth, but that His activities are still going on. God knows no tiredness and He does not need any rest.
The creation of Adam and Eve in heaven was the start of man. Adam and Eve were simultaneously deceived by Satan who tempted them to eat the forbidden fruit. God accepted their repentance, the sin was forgiven and both were sent down to earth.

Sin
All children are born free from sin and if they die during childhood they are sinless and go to live in paradise. Because of this belief there is no place for baptism in Islam.
There are no priests in Islam, instead there are teachers of religion and men of knowledge known as *ulama* (*aalim* in the singular). Every Muslim can lead the prayers at home or in the mosque, or perform any other religious ceremony. Pious Muslims put their trust in God and dedicate their whole life to religion and devotion to God.

Different schools of thought within Islam
There are no major sects within Islam, only different schools of thought. Since all Muslims refer to the same source, the Holy Qur'an, the differences which do occur are generally over details rather than major beliefs and are not important enough to prevent the different schools from marrying or worshipping in the same place.
The two largest schools of thought are the *Sunnis* and the *Shia* and their major difference of opinion is over the succession of the prophet. (The caliphs were appointed as the successors of Muhammad.)
The Shia believe that in every generation there is an Imam who has been divinely appointed and has superhuman qualities. The Sunnis regard the caliph as an ordinary man who has been nominated for his post as head of the community either by his predecessor or by popular vote.

3 How Muslims live

Zakat
Zakat which means purification, is the amount in kind or coins which a Muslim must give to the poor people annually — 2.5 per cent of his savings like gold, silver, money. Land, crops or even cattle has a special rate. However, Muslims are not expected to restrict their charity only to this. Rich or poor Muslims help those in need by giving alms, doing good and offering love and sympathy throughout the year.

The pilgrimage to Mecca
This is a duty for every Muslim, male or female, able, healthy and wealthy enough to perform it once in his life. This holy journey to Mecca must be dedicated entirely to God. To fulfil this duty a Muslim must go to Mount Arafat near Mecca to ask for forgiveness and perform the ritual in the Ka'ba in Mecca at the prescribed time of year.

Pilgrims to Mecca have to circle the sacred Ka'ba seven times

Muslims in Delhi saying prayers to celebrate the ending of Ramadan

Fasting
Fasting is prescribed for Muslims during the month of Ramadan from dawn to sunset. During this period Muslims are not allowed to eat, drink, smoke or have sexual intercourse. The idea behind this is to make the rich feel what the poor feel and to teach Muslims restraint and selfdiscipline. All men, women and children above the age of ten, who are not sick, weak or old and not travelling and can fast must do so every Ramadan.

The Islamic calendar
The Islamic calendar is based on the lunar system. The months are determined by the appearance of the new moon to the naked eye.

This calendar began with the migration of the prophet Muhammad and his his followers from Mecca to Medina, a town which is about 300 miles away from Mecca. This event, known as the *hijra*, took place after the Meccans caused widespread trouble for the followers of the new religion. The year 1969 AD is equivalent to 1389 AH (After Hijra).

Feasts and holidays

Every Muslim should attend the service at the mosque on a Friday. Although all government offices in Muslim countries are closed on that day, it is the busiest day of the week for private business and shops.

Muslims have only a few religious holidays, the birthday of the prophet, the New Year of Hijra, while the two main festivals are *Id-ul-Fitr* and *Id-ul-Adha*.

Id-ul-Fitr is the festival of breaking the fast at the end of Ramadan. It lasts three days and is usually known as the small festival. On the first day in the morning Muslims attend *Id* prayer at the mosque. Before prayers each head of a family must give charity to the poor equivalent to the price of one meal per head of his family. Children wear their new clothes and are given lots of pocket money by all older members of the family and friends which is usually spent on special treats or else saved to buy things like school books, clothes or toys.

During these three days friends visit each other unless they are too far away in which case special festival cards are sent.

Id-ul-Adha is the festival of sacrifice at the end of the pilgrimage to Mecca. It lasts four days and is known as the great festival. On the morning of the first day Muslims attend prayers at the mosque. When they return home, they must (if they can afford it) sacrifice a lamb, cow or camel; the meat should then be given to the poor. This is according to the tradition of the prophet Abraham who sacrificed after he had finished building the Ka'ba at Mecca. The celebrations on this day have not changed since the festival first began.

A typical Id-ul-Fitr card design

Two young Muslims dressed in their best clothes for the Id-ul-Fitr celebrations

Id-ul-Adha prayers at the Shah Jehan mosque in Woking

Marriage and divorce

Both sexes have equal spiritual and civil rights. Marriage is a lifelong union based on an agreement between two individuals, a man and a woman. In this union, each party must have a fair knowledge of the other. This choice must be based first of all on permanent values such as those of faith, morality and devotion. The woman has the right to accept the man or refuse him according to what she desires. The man gives the woman a dowry according to her position in society and to his means. The maintenance of the wife and her children is the duty of the husband even if the woman is wealthy. The marriage must be declared and celebrated in public and at least two Muslim adults have to stand as witnesses.

If this union does not work out, Islam does not force the parties involved to stay together. Divorce is not forbidden but it is not encouraged; it is the last resource after all other means have failed. Divorce is more hateful to God than anything else He permitted as lawful. Either party has the right to seek for divorce but before the final steps are taken certain criteria must be satisfied; both parties must try their utmost to solve the problem; if they fail two arbitrators, one from each side, must be appointed to try to help solve the problem and if this fails the way is free for separation or divorce.

After the divorce there is a waiting time during which neither party is allowed to remarry. This is because time must be allowed for possible reunion in case there is a baby.

Polygamy

Polygamy has been practised throughout human history, but although it is permitted, it is usually limited to a certain degree. It was practised by all civilizations in the east and west.

Polygamy is permitted in Islam if the first wife agrees to it and if the man is willing to treat both wives equally both on an emotional and material basis. As mentioned previously a woman has the right to refuse a man. She also has the right to insist that he signs a contract declaring he will never practise polygamy.

We must remember that polygamy is not imposed by law and is certainly not compulsory but in the case of Islam it is permitted in certain circumstances such as if the wife is not capable of bearing children; if the wife is not capable of intercourse and at certain times especially after war when women outnumber men and there is a liklihood of prostitution. These are general reasons but obviously personal or even political reasons can play a major part in polygamy. With the development or westernization of the Muslim world polygamy today is very rare indeed. It is even forbidden by law in a few countries in the Middle East. If such a law is in the interest of the community the government has the right to impose it provided it does not conflict with religious faith.

Prohibitions
The following things are forbidden for Muslims: alcohol, eating the meat of already dead or strangled animals, pork, lending money on interest, gambling of all kinds, sex in all respects outside marriage, lying, stealing, cheating, murdering and committing suicide. Animals which are to be eaten must be slaughtered in the name of God otherwise the meat is forbidden. The Qur'an allows Jewish and Christian food to be eaten with the exception of pork and alcohol.

Muslims and people of other religions
The Holy Qur'an states: *O people of the scriptures, come to an agreement between us and you that we shall worship none but God, and that we shall ascribe no partner unto Him, and that none of us shall take others for lords besides God.* (Surah 3 v 64)

Muslims are encouraged to strengthen their link with Christians and Jews based on a common religious belief. This belief could provide the good though long overdue basis for better understanding between Muslims and the people of the book i.e. the Bible.

There are three main beliefs common to Islam, Judaism and Christianity. Firstly there is the common belief in the oneness of God. The Qur'an states: *Say: he is God, the one and only. God the eternal, the absolute. He begets not nor is He begotten, and there is none like him.* (Surah 62 v 14) Secondly

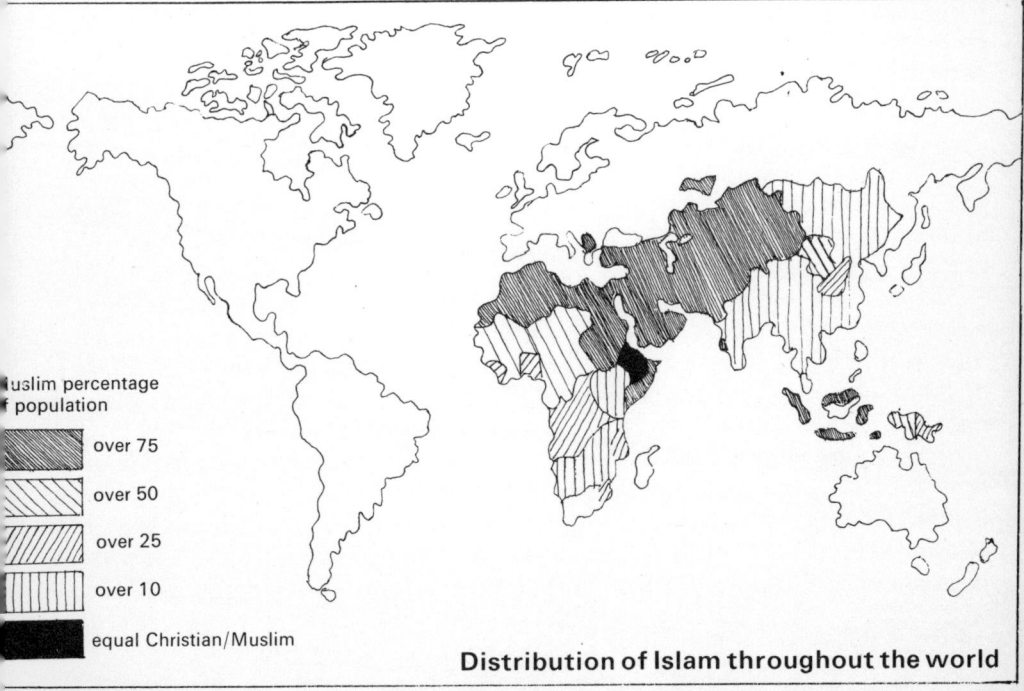

Muslim percentage of population

- over 75
- over 50
- over 25
- over 10
- equal Christian/Muslim

Distribution of Islam throughout the world

there is the belief in the prophets and their messages. The Qur'an states: *Say you: we believe in God and in that which has been sent down on us and sent down on Abraham, Ishmael, Isaac and Jacob and the tribes, and that which was given to Moses and Jesus and the prophets of their Lord. We make no division between any of them and to him we surrender.* (Surah 2 v 136) Thirdly there is the common belief in the brotherhood of mankind. The Qur'an states: *O mankind: we have created you male and female, and have made nations and tribes that ye may know one another. Lo, the noblest of you in the sight of God is he with the best conduct. Lo, God is allknowing, aware.* (Surah 99 v 14)

Suggestions for further reading

M.M. Pickthall *The Meaning of the Glorious Qur'an* New English Library 1964
Abd-al-Rahman Azzam *The Eternal Message of Muhammad* Devin Adair 1964
Dr Hamidullah *Introduction to Islam* Islamic Centre Paris
R. El Droubie *Muslim Point of View of Jesus and Christianity* Minaret House 1968
First Primer of Islam Muslim Educational Trust 1969
Second Primer of Islam Muslim Educational Trust 1969
A.H. Al-Nadwi *Tales of The Prophets* Islamic Book Centre 1969
A. Siddiqi *The Teachings of Islam* Islamic Cultural Centre 1969

All of these books can be obtained from the Islamic Book Centre, 148 Liverpool Road, London N.1.

Index

ablutions 12, 17
Abraham 6, 24
Abu Bakr 8, 20
action 11
angels 9
Arabia
    before Islam 5
archangels 9

belief 9
    shared with other religions 27

calendar, Islamic 23
Christianity 6,7,8,27
creation, story of 21

Day of Judgment 9,11
declaration of faith 12
divorce 26
duties 11
    compulsory to God 12
    towards others 11

fasting 23
feasts 23

Gabriel, angel 8,9,19

Hijra 23
    New Year of 24
holidays 24
holy books 9,11

Id-ul-Adha 24
Id-ul-Fitr 24
Imam 14,16,21
Islam
    and other religions 5,27

beginnings of 5
five pillars of 12
foundations of 9
schools of thought 21

Judaism 6,27

Ka'ba 5,6,7,24
Khadija 7,8

marriage 26
Mecca 5,6,8,13,14,17,23
    pilgrimage to 22,24
Medina 8,23
mosque 13,14,15,17
    women in 17
muezzin 13
Muhammad 5,9,10,11,12,14,19,23,24
    life of 6-8

pillars of Islam, five 12
polygamy 26
prayer 12-16
prohibitions 27

Qur'an 6,9,11,14,17,19-21,27,28
    revelation of 7-8

rak'as 14,16
Ramadan 23

Salat 12
schools of thought 21
Shia 21
sin 21
Sunnis 21

zakat 22